Dragonfly Weather

OTHER TITLES BY LOIS RED ELK

Our Blood Remembers (Many Voices Press, 2011)

Dragonfly Weather

poems · Lois Red Elk

LOST HORSE PRESS
Sandpoint, Idaho

ACKNOWLEDGMENTS

"River Fog," "Solemnity of Wind" and "The Life of Water Spirits" were previously printed in *Yellow Medicine Review* (Spring, 2012).

"I Play a Drum" and "Marriage" were previously published in *Yellow Medicine Review* (Fall, 2012).

"I Am Related to the Day" was published in *Unraveling the Spreading Cloth of Time* (March, 2012).

FIRST EDITION

Cover Art by Michelle Pryor. *Water Dancer,* encaustic with mixed media elements, 12" x 12"
Author Photo by Dennis Minawmish.
Book & Cover Design by Christine Holbert.

This and other Lost Horse Press titles may be viewed online at www.losthorsepress.org.

LIBRARY OF CONGRESS CATALOGING IN PUBLICATION DATA

Red Elk, Lois.
[Poems. Selections]
Dragonfly Weather : poems / Lois Red Elk—First edition.
    pages cm
ISBN 978-0-9883166-5-2 (alk. paper)
I. Title.
PS3618.E4263A6 2013
811'.6—dc23
                              2013021615

CONTENTS

One

Two

Three

Four

Five

This book is dedicated to the
Dragonfly Nation
and to all the Goodhearted Men in the *Tiospaye*—
grandfathers, Red Elk, Grey Bear, High Back & Eagle Plume
father, James
husband, Dennis
sons, Dustin & Neil
grandsons, Jett, Boston & Liam
uncles, Jack, Gerald, Herman & Joe
brother, Russell,
cousins, Jack, Sylvester & Lorne
nephews, James Hart, Russ, Horace, David & Marshall

ONE

"I have been gradually led to believe that the old stories must be taken literally if at all possible, that deep secrets and a deeper awareness of the complexity of our universe was experienced by our ancestors, and that something of their beliefs and experiences can be ours once again."

—Vine Deloria, Jr., *God Is Red*

ANCIENT STORYTELLER

This story of water, sun, and the one with four wings
began ages ago when one of the oldest storytellers
on earth, the Dragonfly, reminded me of its journey.
Traveling south through portals of D/Lakota culture,
I asked layers of sediment to sift away for this quest
I needed. I went back to my life of neutrinos and
prayed my way up through the layers of sparks and
connections to the life of the woman of this century.
I searched among my traditional relatives whose
spirits dwell in the royal dust of the vermilion rock
trail and hunted beyond graves and mastodon bones
to the blood of those who sacrificed and pledged
tobacco offerings for all who escaped the fire.
Dragonfly's life was created to exist for eons and
to surface only when water and sun agreed to bring
forth their best cradle—a bath of tepid marsh. To
the south where I met the full radiance of the sun,
many ancient Nations welcomed me, shook my hand
and invited heavy rain clouds to witness our meeting.
They watched as sun sent a scattering of sacred rocks
to be recognized and carried back to my homelands.
The rocks were perfectly round and in the likeness
of the sun—shielding my eyes from exposure.
When home, I placed the rocks in the water and
watched the coming of larvae elongating for a
smooth flow through air. It was the four-winged
storyteller. Stories emerged that told of their
beginning, the silent watery home that protected
them, about a life of utmost speed where their
playing with hail is a game, how they shared their
energy with humans, that they may be swift in their
stride and in making serious decision. Through
dreams the D/Lakota saw that Dragonfly had special
powers that allowed it to evade stones of ice, and
because of this, for protection against arrows and

bullets the D/Lakota decorated their shields with images of hail and dragonflies. It was the mothers and grandmothers who fashioned brightly painted dragonflies into the design of moccasins to allow the youth a fast run. Uncles painted dragonflies on the flanks of horses to aid speed and a quick escape from those who brought harm. The teachings received from Dragonfly are many and are shared by many tribal people. The life of Dragonfly is short, but their lessons and blessings last forever. They remind us not to waste time, but to live life fully. When all seems lost, Dragonfly's power grants redemption from dark thoughts to clear thinking at the speed of light. The knowledge among these pages is from the D/Lakota culture. It is passed on for the benefit of the children, the sick, and the weary. All people are to gain from the teachings of the flying ones. They traveled for millions of years to be with us. With the blessings of the Dragonfly Nation we share.

DRAGONFLY'S OFFERING

Up from the roots of frog's mud a forceful strength
    is watching
green willows surge and fill with moments of
    lightning. Straight
stems elongate from earth saliva for a life of ritual
    to become
an abode of shelter and womb for embryo
    transformations. A peeking
sun waiting for gaping throats, asks opal eggs to
    make an offering
before they swallow waves of intense heat for their
    growth. Beating
hearts cluster in opaque clots of eggs. Their in-
    sync movement is a
music determined to cling to reeds among quiet
    water surrogates.
More pleas to the gods of light to open clouds and
    allow warm rays
to surround webbed bubbles as they emerge from
    life. In Dragonfly's
ebbing dreams he feels the force of water, strange
    moments of storm,
and a place he thinks he remembers. They stir his
    fluid body in
throbbing movement. He recalls this new life from
    a different time, a place of unity
with tornado, hail and storm. He feels the pull of
    membranes wanting
to unfold and take shape, experiences a quickness
    of air, a reprieve from

growing pains needing relief. Ancestor apparitions
   of various stations
      surge his space with waves of heat turning water
         into warm birthing
      places. He welcomes the coming of another life
         with the wind. In
      Dragonfly's new vision, he asks what his offering
         to earth will be.

SOLEMNITY OF WIND

for my brother, Russell

Send me the drumming hoof beats from a
    low thunder off today's early sunrise, while
    a deep azure wind prepares for the entities
that will transform into their mature lives.

I want to watch as wind escorts all the invited
    associate gods who will participate and support
        this sacred ritual where relatives of the earth
announce a reciprocal passion for all birth.

I yearn to see the rising dust made by the
    hooves of excited horses as pellets of
        rainwater and flaring nostrils loosen
energy from full clouds for this occasion.

I wish to inhale fresh ions from the breath of the
    four directions as the circling wind is welcomed.
        Laugh with me when gathered lightning binds
my hands to the mane of my roan stallion.

I need to ride with the hail and dragonflies for
    the endurance of this parade. I want to watch
        as earth trembles to the ancient music of the
horse's electric song stirring hills with sudden growth.

Let me witness the unfolding of life from a quiet,
    dormant place into the strength of a mighty circle.
        Let my spirit keep time with the beat that rain
makes awaking the entities that will dance and surround.

This season has arrived through the winged power
    that makes all things move. I want to attest
      as the competent wind unites its power with
waiting waters and births a single spirit for the water spout.

And, it is for all to see the incubated and eagerly waiting
    whirlwind as it finally grabs the sky, then surprises
      dry dust with a circle dance that unites the gods
above with the gods below for this seasons encore.

THEIR PRAYER FOR RAIN

He offers an eagle wing and draws a circle where the
    sky and earth create a bond. It is the plea from
        many hearts and tongues, and his longing, that will call
    creator's attention for responding signs.
    In between deep breaths and songs, a ring will
        gently vibrate among old river banks where ponds,
           dry skin, and silent grasses join
the request.

She offers up bowls of cedar and eases into the
    skin of silent prayers where depth of knowledge comes
        from mother's womb. Her prayer tongue, turning into
    many languages, awakens all spirits who will watch for
    a smoke offering, and listen for the beat of
ancient water songs.

Lizard instructs with tracks leading into the shadows of
    gathering clouds. He remembers creation and his
        agreement to guard the cascades. His lodge between
    rocks and sun turns into sweat as he carves his
    composition in sand and asks for final direction
        to lay his dying offspring, or to lay his dependents
in future pools.

Rushing to the camp of all those making a plea, brown and
    scorched leaves tumble, while furry, parched relatives offer
        tufts of sweet grass from subterranean altars.
    Then coyote, lifting his scruffy head, speaks with the apparitions
    in a surprising, but pleasing melody, lamenting his thirst and
        and dry tongue. And, it is his simple song that draws
appeased clouds across the plains.

REWARDS OF THE WESTERN GODS

for nephew, James Hart

It could be the raging obscure formations
     rotating flaying arms of mist, power shifting
     seasonal air into a downpour of drowning water,
         or it could be the blinding bolt fastening

waiting heavens to a shivering cold purple earth.
     It could have been the screams of thunder's
     gaping beaks that prompted the delicate four-
         winged into an ultimate frenzy of aerobatic

dance moves. But it wasn't. Honored to play
     with the West's finest winds, the playful
     dragonfly maneuvered easily with every surging
         deluge, with every forceful outburst the West could

throw. It was time to fill sere pods and thirsting roots,
     time to restore shrunk beds of rivers, and dust-
     filled edges of aching, cracked soil. The waning moon
         looked at the pulse of hidden life and let the well fill.

Grandfather stated, It is the power of the West's black wind,
     cover your head, bow, chant prayers, light sage and cedar.
     Your thirst will drink of generous clouds. Grateful you stand
     remembering the rewards of the Western gods.

RIDING OUT OUR MORTALITY

I look at the veil like wings of your lift
and flight, the stratus of dawn reflecting
in your eyes, and I believe that it was in
the sediment that we survived the fall
of giants, ash of fires, and drowning flood.
We were always children of the western
gods, the power of whirlwind, motion
the circular of cocoons; the ultimate
power of earth's rotating winds. Those
gods held us close as the fire-might in
earth erupted and radiant blasts from
the third direction sent out a ring of fire.
We remember the rumblings of earth's
interior lives, the same fires of the sun.
We witnessed the birthing of distant
spires as they grew toward the stars. It
was an example to assure our
longevity, our ability of flight and grace.
We never forgot our visit to the warm
swamps and hushed waters during our
early beginnings, the moist soil and
damp caverns of our birth. It was we
who were thankful for this alien travel
to unite with the globe of mist, the
timing of heat and love of caring
grasses. You were much larger then,
wings the length of my body, all-
knowing eyes that reeled my skull,
your six gentle hands that busied our
food and studied the foliage with song.
We replied in our own tongues, prayers
for the event, for the growth of place as
our common mother lifted her bosom to
embrace the blue mist and steam that

leaned into our growth and flight. Our years were millions, now we count summers for our new lives. And we are still here, riding out our mortality.

They say in the old time stories that when Dragonfly lived with the giants, he had a wing span over five feet wide.

ALL THIRST QUENCHED

for granddaughter, Wahcawin

I didn't want to scold the sky that year, but
Grandma's words taunted my senses. If there
is a thirst, then you need to pity the flowers

in a loud voice. Ask the frogs why they are
being punished, stomp on the ground and talk
to the dried clay about cracking open the earth.

I know challenging the storm is risky. "Last
but not least, burn cedar and pray the lightning
doesn't strike your town." That night, the stars

disappeared, so did the birds. Perhaps it was
the season for rain or the dance. In the western
distance, we thought we heard cannon blasts,

looking over we watched the horizon fill with
lightning strikes. Rain couldn't pour hard enough
over the thirsty plain. Accompanying clouds,

called to thunder's voice in extreme decimals
requesting all the water heaven could send forth,
to come. Rain and more rain filled empty stream

bottoms. Rivers who had pulled their dry banks
farther and farther from their center begged for
a drink to startle dusty beds with a flooding roar.

Lives in dormant places begin to stir and awaken
The lives of water beings, those that swim, the
ones that hop, and the ones that fly, begin to stir.

That year all thirst was quenched.

HEHAKA WAKPA

for grandson, Boston

Elk River we call it, the sweet
    tasting sips of sky,
a slip of music slicing its way
    across mature earth,
filling cleavage with water
    tasting of elk songs.
The male four-legged's bugle,
    quench their thirst, and
leave strands of their voice
    in places of repose, where
the strength and calm of Mother's
   flowing cup vibrates our senses
    from warm earth to rest,
leaving us at banks with moist skin
    wanting to dip
    a hand in the river and
    retain *Hehaka's* blessing
for our memory.
    At this time of settling,
    the river wishes a good night
to summer, and reaches
  for the axis of winter's pull.
Grandmother prepares the children
    for bed and sends them
the fluid melody of elk songs
    to help us cross into
restful places of our dreams.
    As we close our eyes,
we pray the waters also rest,
    travel slowly under ice, then
warm their flow for
    the next rotation of earth.

Hehaka Wakpa: Elk River or Yellowstone River

RIVER FOG

Grandfather's breath
           slips silently
over the water,
     a visible prayer
renewing
     this old water
          since time
               was infant.

I hear little,
          but watch
all, receive with
     open arms,
          branches reaching,
          reeds lifting,
          river letting go
               of fog in a slow exhale.

My skin
          too,
     crawled from the mud,
          breathes
with open pores
          after
               the subtle dew,
glistening, refreshed.

Then we behold
           the moving one,
     quietly and
     thankfully
     observe
          as he lifts,
               dissolves,
                    departs.

MOTHER'S WATER

it is always the water first
    trickling down mature legs
coming from an interior source
    where mist inhabits stomach caves
where a pool collects all droplets
    upon the arrival of the first blood
where ache signals the flow and
    Mother Earth in her longing
to keep creation a learned ritual
    propels the human river to live
where her streams are my arteries
    her veins set off my streams
her rivers are my amniotic flow
    Earth's possession, her ancient body,
renews self in my flooding moon
    against the moisture of the womb
where she shared her cradle, became
    my womb, my place in cosmos,
in creation, together they passed on
    the power of conception, of birthing
life again with the permission of
    Mother's all sacred flowing waters

DRAGONFLY MEDICINE

for nephew, David

Rain bounces off a tightly stretched deer skin
    attached to a frame of bone and wood,
a skip of downward energy hitting in
                time with pulse.
Inside the circular space of air I hear a faint
    vibration of aorta and vein as the hushed
roar of wave after wave slips into the
                core for tone.
The beat of wings passes through many songs,
    seeps up throats, peering out the
closed eyelids of entranced drummers, their
                voice of visions.
Medicine is lit, smoke travels far to the south
    beckoning all still forms to rise, shake
out old energies, inhale the swarming fog,
                offer an opening.
Dance in dragonfly style, dodge dangers thrown,
    dare a step with lightning strike.
Your life is protected by drum of water—
                dragonfly medicine

TWO

"Man's heart away from nature becomes hard."

—*Standing Bear*

LIVING WITH MONSTERS

It's hard living with monsters. These are real.
They seem to have replaced that spot in every
empty family. Any future thoughts about

where excessive bad habits would lead, does not
exist. After awhile the monster turns into many,
so many there comes a time when one cannot look

at self. Mirrors become monsters who peer back.
When the family sneaks a look they find a way to
ignore what they see. But, that isn't the end; they

start to dream about bigger monsters that haunt
their day times as well. It is just a matter of time
before someone or something else is blamed for the

monsters. Soon they deny they have anything to do
with monsters. It is the best way to get past facing
what they have given their life for. When they run

out of money, feeding monsters, household items
start to disappear—the toaster, a pair of shoes, or
the kid's dream catcher. Of course it is blamed on

keeping the monsters away. One day they wake up
and find they have lost a beloved cousin, but couldn't
be at the funeral because they were running away

from monsters. The police report in the newspaper
says there was a call, an arrest. The charge? Disorderly
conduct, fighting with monsters. Family and friends

say they have done all they can, they pray for help,
pray all the monsters will go away. Their medicine
man tells them to stop suffering and have some faith.

"Suffering houses monsters, faith houses hope."

HER KIND OF WATER

Bright red and swollen, her face is a map of the struggles
she bears from those who have turned their backs on her.
She wakes on Hangover Road every morning and makes

the painful walk to town. She must leave before the others
wake up. It's a game of cat-and-mouse. Her best hiding
place, the safest place, is the streets, in full sight, where no

one will strike and take what little she has left. I always
see her on the first of the month, planning her dodging
game. The street people know she is *cashie* and they

all require a few dollars from 'Cousin.' Now it's the
end of the month, she is broke and shaky, needing a
few dollars for her thirst. This morning she stands on

the corner by the food store hoping someone dashing in
to get rolls and eggs for breakfast will take pity on her.
She scans the parking lot for a potential target and sees

an old childhood friend, remembers a joke they shared,
a possible opening to talk, to laugh, to make the painful
decision to ask for some spare change, enough for coffee.

Her friend is a descendant of chiefs, from the Horse Clan.
Their upbringing is to share, even if it's a cup of water,
the last piece of bread, or what little soup is leftover.

Their eyes meet. One, an appeal for mercy, the other
an honest smile. They shake hands, share a few words
and as the friend finds her keys, she gives five dollars.

Just one kind gesture, one moment of acceptance as
one human to another was all that was needed. Her
kind of water that day was water, sweet, sweet, water.

. . . NUMB, BUT WALKING

Again, a party of them are dragging their bodies up and
down the street, sizing up the south-end houses
to see who is home, who could be a possible target.
They darken and hinder doorways using the frame
to hold up bodies that want so desperately to collapse,
an effort opposing that intoxicating dose that wants to melt
them away into an alcohol pool somebody will pay attention to.
They use limp, doubled-up fists to beat the wooden door
like a woodpecker gone haywire, a kind of senseless,
uneven tempo, their drunken calling card.
When no one answers, a slow motion language is uttered,
so slurred it sounds foreign. We think only their kind understands.
Names of people are called out who don't exist anymore,
a desperate plea, as if beckoning the dead could open doors.
If no one answers, that is when the craziness begins.
A cold weather extension cord hanging off the wall outlet
is yanked out and carried off.
Or a rake is dragged away, scraping so loud the screeching
echoes down the block, enough to wake the dead.
All the noise stirs the local dogs. Now it's time to call the police.
It's a series of events any can imagine. The guard dog,
mouth wide and foaming, jumps into action.
A newly planted tree is yanked out of the earth and
turned into a sword maneuvered in slow motion.
The dog leaps, but backs away from the sense of so much withering.
The neighbors holler out, threaten, then break out in laughter.
Children seated on bikes have a ringside seat, more real than TV.
The soused came for something: some hope for open doors, but
when no one responds, they take anything, just to be getting.
It makes them feel like they pulled the wool over eyes that should care.
Someone has been watching all along and have an exact description.
That one, only his alcoholism has been known since his youth.
Eventually the police arrive, catch one of them and
return all the stolen stuff.
There have been many official written police complaints.
"They looked so tired, like numb . . . but walking."

THE HAPPY MAGPIE

I remember those times from my youth when mean words
hurt so much I wanted to cry. My dear, fierce aunt saw my
face one day and asked what was wrong. After telling her
about the mean girls and their mean words, she looked hard
at me and gave me a story I will never forget. She said, In
every town on this rez one can find magpies sitting on sagging
fences looking for some good piece of trash to dig into. In
her language they are called *unk-ce'k ih'a,* or they 'eat feces
laughing.' She asked me, Did you ever watch a magpie, how
they enjoy themselves after they feed? They tilt their heads
back and cackle. So full of whatever garbage they can pick
around in, so anxious to throw their voices into the air and let
go all the foul breath they can exhale. "Doesn't this remind
you of gossipers?" I guess gossip could be considered trash.
Most sensible two-legged throw out all their trash because it
either smells or it's of no use. I do know that gossip is either
made up or an outright lie. To me that is trash. Long time ago,
we told stories that had a moral or an important lesson that
needed to be shared. Some of our old stories were told to us
by the animals, especially *Iktomi,* the trickster. But the kind
of stories gossipers spread around have no moral standards,
no cultural value, no hint of truth at all. Auntie said, Now you
watch, the mornings seem to be the best time to start looking
for the biggest dump, to ingest, belch out, throw back their
heads and cackle. Auntie gave me some sage, she told me to
put it in my pockets. Sage wards off evil and will protect
your dear heart. And remember, she said, what makes a happy
magpie or a happy gossiper? It's the same thing. They both
have to ingest crap to thrive, to make themselves happy.

FENCES

Memory doesn't hold the experience
when it became right to fence the earth.
Father told of the time a corner post
was erected at the edge of his land. He
saw farmers use their maps, trucks, wire
and might. Leaning and pulling, they
stretched barbed wire around acres of
tumbleweed and sage. They said it was
to keep the cows in, but it was to keep
the Indians from having access to the river
while the cows wasted the water. They
called us neighbors, neighbors who
were the losers, but who were hungry
enough to know how to kill and butcher
a cow in half an hour. Dad and his
cousins used the corner post to stake out
the cow, the fence to dry the cowhide,
then the hide to wrap and pack the meat.
Two kinds of sagebrush were liberated
to cover the smell of blood, and getting
caught. Only tell-tale sign was the
buzzard hawk circling down entrails
not buried deep enough. Farther on
down the river we washed our hands
of all that was wrong that day.

THE DEAD HAVE GATHERED

The dead have gathered all
    their spirits and departed.
They now know more about
    creation's beauty than what
was pretended by those who
    lied to us. They leave us
with what we thought was
    comfort—with a replacement,
not our spiritual birthright, even
    though we still possess our
sacred selves. The dead do not
    miss our misery, but see with-
in our whole spirits what we have
    always been, they know
us the way we were meant to be,
    the way we were birthed.
They see only the goodness
    of our earthly lives, one we
knew as children, the life that
    still exists, but was hidden from
our souls, replaced with strange
    ideas and unimaginable rules,
confusing, threatening and
    starving our poor spirits.
They pray for us and reach out
    for our prayers. Some respond
and are nourished, but some
    can't reach and find induced
sleep their only comfort.

TAKE HER HANDS

Female whole, but losing ground,
    standing there weeping
and screaming her loss.
It was like the sun and the moon left
        her alone on an isolated star,
her voice failing, her arms flaying,
    I thought she would fall over
from the vanishing of breath.
            Her body swayed in a
circular motion, an angle
        the force of anguish.
Loving feelings, so precious

                        leaving

and out of reach.
    Suicide thoughts
taking over all her senses,
    all stability.
                Her knife slashes her arms.
"You with the beaded moccasins,
    take her hands," shouted my aunt,
"Bring her back,
    she needs to think clearly."

It was our way of showing support,
sharing her grief that she must
    continue with the earth for now,
        to remember the living.
                And, it was enough
to give her composure,
        to let her know, why she had to stay.

"Take her hands" are words Sioux women say when someone is overwhelmed.

FISH BUTTE

It happens every time I look deep into the dark
turbid water of *Mini Sose*. View is the sure
control and determined flow of life with one
direction. There is no pity or pause for those
who disrespect or foolishly slip into its pathway.
The enormous energy forced by age-old memory,
pulled by gravity and call of Mother's ancient
ocean songs, is the urgent motion of its life, to
churn with sand and cleanse earth. The power
brings forth female legends of foreboding and
promise, to remind and solve. I listen and learn,
then recall and recite the rewards of lessons hard
learned. A message was carried to us from those
ancestors who met the giant sturgeon in the time
before they knew legs, when we swam with the
salamanders and lizards. I give my water spirit
to the river and learn the language of water. Easier
now to translate fear into the kindness of swimming.
Easier now to change words into the power of gills.
Easier now to disassemble wanton thoughts for the
ancient spirit within. It was how the two-legged
treated the poor and the different, that began the
cleansing cycle. Those who were slow, lame or
old, those who could not help themselves were
ousted and left to fend, to scratch the earth, and
suffer freezing snow, baking sun, and harsh winds.
Tears from all ages flowed from the mistreatment
of these pitiful. Tears so fluid, so sad they entered
the river and created eddies of despair amidst the
listening flow of water apparitions. A young man
visiting his brother by the river cried at the condition
of his village when suddenly the river began to rise
and shudder. It threw waves as high as the nests in
the cottonwoods. The men were frightened and prayed.

The giant water monster who was listening to their sad story, asked the men to be calm and listen to his message. I know your situation, I have a plan. When all the people are asleep, tell your friends, tell the weak, old and poor to gather at one end of the village, then come to the river's edge and call for me. During the night one of the old ones heard strange sounds and became alarmed and wanted to run away. This alerted all the people that the river spirit had awakened the giant sturgeon. Everyone started to shout and scatter. Still hoping that the plan could work, the young men ran to the river's edge to call for help. Suddenly the water began to churn and splash. Waves grew higher and higher. A great roar was heard as the giant flew up on the bank. Astonished at the size, the young men were thrown back. They watched as the fish waddled back and forth across the land raising dust, creating a deep furrow across the land. Finally it reached the village and laid down in a half circle like a quarter moon, then rolled and rolled till all the mean and greedy people were killed. Just as his tail and head were about to meet, the young men led all the poor people out of the circle to escape. All the belongings and storage bins of food were saved, to be given to the needy. All night the giant fish crawled across the prairie. In the morning the people followed the trail and found the fish had dried up into the shape of a butte. This butte still stands on the prairie as a reminder to all greedy and cruel people.

20 TOBACCO TIES

Again, the *Wakanyeja* have brought us
together. In the December moon, blood
was spilled among the innocent. I see
them holding hands and growing wings
for their journey back to the Creator,
their souls now know only the beauty and
love of the Great Spirit. First I take my
birch bark basket, filled with tobacco,
and place it next to the buffalo skull altar,
then twenty pieces of red cloth are prepared in
small squares. As each square is filled with
tobacco, prayers are made to the Maker
of us all to travel with the innocents on
their journey to the heavens. Their walk
here was brief and in beauty, now the
Great Mystery has received their young, pure
lives back to paradise. They will dance
in eternity with the souls who have gone ahead.
Choirs of ancestors and angels lift their
voices in song to welcome them to the
realm of grace. Those left on earth will
go on, with tears of unbearable sadness,
precious memories, and lessons to unravel.

Wakanyeja: Sacred beings, children

BEARING WITNESS

for my sister, Iris

Upon receiving the Cobell check, I'm taken back to
my youth on the flats of the Chelsea Community where
twenty Sioux families lived on the Ft. Peck Reservation.

My sister, Iris and I, only three and four-years-old in our long,
brown, cotton stockings and woolen bonnets withstood
the cold of a November ground wind as we walked across

the prairie to our auntie's house for an emergency visit.
We, to play with our first cousins, our parents, distressed.
These adult eyes become the eyes of a child looking at

the love and togetherness and faith in our dear *tiospaye*.
But, this time, Father and Mother were very upset over some-
thing that happened. They and the uncles and grandpas

had a meeting to talk, to work out something together.
Later in my life, as an adult, I would be educated about
the efforts of the adults back then, how hard they tried.

And, I would eventually piece together the puzzle to
learn of the crooked deals made by the BIA. Our land
was stolen, our livestock rustled or killed, our leases

unfair or no lease even existing. The land was farmed
without tribal people knowing. Someone was getting rich.
Today I received a $1,000 dollar check, and asked myself,

can this money take away the stress, the sadness and
the anger executed upon my parents and family. They have all
since passed away and know nothing of this settlement.

But I remember. I remember them in my heart and I
send prayer smoke to the spirits in honor of their lives.
They survived despite the schemes to cheat them of what

was rightfully theirs. I am here today as evidence of our
survival, I thank them for taking care of us in the best
way they could. I am here to bear witness to their lives.

Tiospaye: immediate and extended family

THREE

"The wind, in its greatest power, whirls. Birds make their nest in circles, for theirs is the same religion as ours . . ."

—*Black Elk*

DRAGONFLY WEATHER

This Earth has always belonged to those who love her and
recognize her as the revered elder of motion. *Maka Unci*
(Grandmother Earth) and *Maka Ina* (Mother Earth) we have

called her. The Dreams that were sent to our beloved
ancestors told us to *Makoce wayanka* (view the land) as
our flesh, and follow her example, guide the life of all those

who birthed our blood, winter after winter throughout all
time. Our people remember the grandeur of our creation
songs, when the Divine gave us rock, the winds, water, the

beings of the earth, and the beautiful flowers of plants.
We named them *Inyan, Tate, Mini, Wamakaskan,* and
maka etanhan taku icaga. We knew we were related to

everything, because we are all made of the same that is of
earth. In our visits with all earthly things we learned to
love all that was given to us. The earth and all her living

creations never lied to us. We learned to trust her and all
her relatives, the sky, the moon, sun and stars, and we
recognized them as the relatives above. The four-legged, the

beings that fly, and all the beings that live with water spoke
the same language as our own. They helped us through
the seasons, gave our bodies energy, and spoke to us about

the spirits that dwell in all of us and in creation. Long ago
the D/Lakota wisdom instructed us to share. Share food,
share wealth, share responsibility, share the earth, share

the connection to the animals, share the beauty of prayer,
and share the teachings. This is the time—the season when
all seems lost—to pick up your heart, and give it to the Great

Mystery. The rotation of our star, the plants, and the animal messengers all believe in the Great Mystery. Pick up the culture and the wise stories for our safety, enlightenment

and health. Who will we listen to? Pick a season and the plants and animals will choose you. The wolf teaches about family, the bear teaches medicine, the turtle teaches us to

care for the children, and the dragonfly teaches us to be swift in worth. This is the season, the time of dragonflies, when we need to leave harm, make swift decisions, escape

quickly to the good world, when our star is aligned with sun, when plants and water incubate beginnings of being, of wings, for earth life. When the earth, through female

water, births the messenger of the necessary, the need to find value, the essence of your being will open the heart to the new season. This is Dragonfly weather.

TUSWECA, WANA HI

Daku Shkah Shkah. All day a movement
                (in my language) led me away from the usual
like something familiar had jumped eagerly into my space
                and agreed to push me forward.
Short hours took hold, passed me mindlessly
                through clouds as sun descended.
                        Drifting home I kept looking at an anxious sky,
the trees, and my pace in this world.
                All became a unified motion in play,
a decoding of sidewalks allowed me to float   one limb at a time
        across town.   I was kept in a hurried westerly direction,
                streetlights wired to pass me on. Overhead, a dark vortex,
rotating flying objects,   took on a life of their own.
Particles of leaves, twigs and dying weeds
                floated back and forth.
As I neared my street an old lesser breeze enveloped my body
                                and took control of my bearings.
All appeared in harmony,   like a secret plan going well, while
        I seemed to be shaking hands with the wind
                but needing to find the brace of trees—the anchor of roots.
As I climbed the stairs   an aroused sky took hold
                and drew a hard rain close.
Relieved to be on the porch before the storm,
I saw a large shaded ancestor   dart and duck through debris
        kicked up by the motion   as if in fun, like a game of tag.
                Tusweca, wana hi, Dragonfly has arrived.
                        In awe I watched large four wings
        maneuver through gusts   with so much ease and
                joy it looked to be putting on a show of its
flying talents. Now the swift messenger was involving
        me in its space, charging, and challenging an exchange.
                In a flash it thwarted me, eye to eye, and then
        swerved off into the hail and pounding rain.
I sensed playfulness   yet a power only the assured can throw.
I felt an urge to dance   in the warm rain,   to take flight

as if I could.   Hard and fast as hail hit the ground,
          the ghost-like four wings, (one of the gifts from
the thunder gods)   outmaneuver the ice rocks.   In its flight
I understood the need for speed
          and realized the day's journey was in preparation
for this valuable knowledge—the power of movement.

Daku Shkah Shkah: that which makes everything move.
Tusweca, wana hi: Dragonfly has arrived.

THE SKY IS A SECRET PATH

The sky is a secret path
  for all birds
    who believe in maps.
        They soar and bite off
        pieces of blue and orange sky
        for wings.
They argue
  with rain as feathers ride
    the back of a silent wind and
      turn their breath into clouds.
        You and I don't hear
        their language as it circles
        among the electric plugs
        that connect kites and
        planes to another voice line.
We only wish
  for wings,
    for the lift into the wash
      of flower spirits arching a rainbow
      across our home.
        The sky is a secret journey
        for all who chance
        an exciting undertaking,
        to take a breath for a
        rising updraft.
Our hopeful hearts,
  become rapid drumbeats
    as we reach
      into all dimensions
      of the secret sky.

MY GRANDDAUGHTER'S BEADED PURSE

We decided to stop at Tule Creek and look for mint tea.
Mom said the fragrance was strong along this side of the
hills. We all piled out of the car. My son and my oldest

granddaughter were anxious as we stepped onto the gravel
road. We followed Mom's lead along the low hills. The
wind was blowing hard, specks of dust and straw floated

into our hair. Granddaughter turned to me avoiding the
dust. She said giant flies were buzzing around her. Mom
stopped, scanning the tall grasses along the creek, I could

sense she had picked up the sweet aroma of mint. We all
stopped, amazed at the scent flowing our way.
Suddenly the wind slowed, Mom pointed and hurried in the

direction of flies. Again, Granddaughter said the flies were
giant ones. Mom pointed to one and said *They are called
dragonflies and like to fly with the wind.* She said they

were welcoming her. They were glad she was here. Mom
picked some mint, but the water was too deep. She said it
was okay, that what she got was enough. She said a quiet

prayer, then said a storm was coming. We quickly returned
to the car. Granddaughter sat in front with Mom. As we
started down the road, Mom looked back at me and said in

Dakota, *Look at this. Look what is riding with us.* She
spoke in Dakota so as not to startle Granddaughter. A large
purple and blue dragonfly was sitting on the dashboard. I

asked Granddaughter if she liked the giant flies. She said
they were pretty. I told her one of them wants to ride along
with us and pointed. She turned, smiled, then looked back at

me. The dragonfly rode with us till we reached home, then flew out the door. We told Granddaughter that this was a happy time. My mother had practiced her culture for us that

day. She knew it was the right time to show us her traditions. We witnessed the power of her belief in the shape of hills, the power of wind over the land, the message of dragonflies, and

how to find mint. Later that summer, my granddaughter's beaded purse was created to mark the time, the story of a visit with Grandma. It is a Dakota design: summer flowers and a

dragonfly. Colors from the four winds take their place with earth and mint. It symbolizes a blessing for her walk with an elder great-grandma. A promise was kept to teach the children.

LIVING FAIRYTALE BOOK

for granddaughter, Isanti

"We are little birds in a nest, waiting for the warmth
of mother's return, wanting the morsels, the sustenance."
I still hear Grandmother's voice; a section of DNA spliced

over my ears, translating through my elk tooth earrings,
an echo off her badlands. Her everyday language was my
poetry, lived in mind's eye. I heard decibels floating

through gray matter in the colors of earth's palate.
She was a living fairytale book, soothing in the Hunkpapa
tongue, sliding the 'L' with a pause for distinction, the

music of ancient beginnings. Her mouth vibration
expressed the fullness of antlers and trees. Her eyes
relayed images of her participation with the four-legged,

some standing on two, others related by genesis from
stories sent through spider's web. The stories always
ended with lessons from all the relatives, from the caves

(sentences in shapes of essence), from the rocks (heated to
lava pouring from the veins of the blue woman), from the
tattoos (following her design in stars and molecules),

from stories of dragonflies, horses, lightening, and the
giant sturgeon. Nothing would escape her ear, her vision.
Lifting her arms and waving her hands in circles, seeking

endorsement from the sky, she would slide a hand towel
across her moist forehead, wet with exhausting belief
that her language was alive.

THE ROUND HOUSE

for my uncles, Gerald and Herman

Bodies as essence, whole, merge through bright
welcoming doors, the portals into the sanctity
    of the round house.
The interior, the course of our lives in constant
circular motion, to guide us among the seasons,
    ages, and time memorial.
Grandmothers with shawls, blankets and bundles
of plenty, followed by joyful children, little hands
    in tight fists around
flowing fringes that sway off the backs of tall
graceful women. Their hair, black and waist-length,
    share music of small
tinkling shells tied off the ends of neatly braided
strands. Sweet smoke fills the air and floats near
    the dome's wooden planks,
a walkway to the ghost road, the northern star and
the seven sisters. They too are welcome here as we
    exchange same spirit.
Our grandfathers prepare to unite all those who have
come for this time of reverence. I see them kneeling
    in the center of the floor,
gently laying out the sacred pipes, then with more care,
tying eagle plumes on branches. I'm seated close to
    Grandma, hear her softly
hum an accompaniment to the low beat of the drum
across the room, learned in the womb, tongue pulses
    like the heartbeat.
She knows the ritual, the common sharing of their
united rhythm, a flow of human bonding for what
    they believe.
These walls absorb smoke of sage and cedar, absorb
pleas and gratefulness for prayer. The air is filled
    with spirits that vibrate

off all the hearts, and turns the house into a womb of
safety, pure love, worship, and renewal. I snuggle
        closer to Grandma, rest
my head on her arm, feel the warmth, a cushion of
love and joy, like she'd be there forever and ever, for
        my memories and support.
It was at that moment, in our sacred round house that
I knew I was forever connected to the spirituality
        of ancestral blood.

SILENT LIFE LETTING GO

Frozen creek beds shift,
  fall apart
    little by little
  ice and snow
      exchanging
lives to become
    trickling water
for the beginning
  reach of hair like wood
    living deep
deep under the trunk
    of glowing tree buds.
Clouds off the river,
  a steam, like breath
    extending
for sun releasing
  mud into frogs.
Earth stretching
  after winter sleep
    for grizzlies
    exhaling old breath
      of hibernation.
Sun warming air
    for geese reaching
  for flight and
    wings leaving
  equator.
  Silent life letting go,
for the arc
    of a new sun.

SOMETIMES *ODOWAN*

Sometimes when I sleep,
I hear buffalo coming,
Sometimes when I sleep,
Tatanka sings me songs.
Hey yo hey yaaaaah.

Sometimes when I dream,
I see dragonflies flying.
Sometimes when I dream,
Tusweca sings me songs.
Hey ya hey yaaaaah.

Sometimes when I wake,
I feel the earth moving.
Sometimes when I wake,
Maka Unci sings me songs.
Hey ya hey yaaaaah.

Sometimes when I walk,
I smell the river tumbling.
Sometimes when I walk,
Mini Sose sings me songs.
Hey ya hey yaaaaah.

Tatanka: A buffalo and an ancient relative
Tusweca: A dragonfly and is born in water.
Maka Unci: The earth and our grandmother
Mini Sose: The Missouri river and means turbulent water

THE LIFE OF WATER SPIRITS

Tonight I watch churning water loosen
         wandering pebbles
     clinging to tender sand as
Mini Sose rages and playfully laughs
    in all her fullness
       on her continuous journey
below overhanging cottonwoods.
Nearby a cloudy cobalt mist
      flutters above stirring eddies,
   while moonlight reaches and
    kisses the larger stones.
My skin senses a restless water spirit
     within my breath lift and follow
in unison with all the water spirits
      who have echoed their voices
    between these banks for
thousands and thousands of years.

Mini Sose: Missouri River and turbid water

TAH-TEY (WIND)

It happened last night in a dream. The winds
urged me to write them a poem. The request
didn't come like a whisper or a roaring tornado.
It was a humming at a distance above leaves,
a perfect note, not discernible in any language,
holding in *a cappella,* they wouldn't stop long
enough to sit and tell me one of their best stories.

I didn't want to write about the bad news I
had been hearing—that huge tornadoes destroyed
so many little towns in Oklahoma and Kansas, that
it brought deathly freezing wind across the high
plains, that it kicked up the dust and clouded the
Arizona skies. I wanted to hear the truth of why
it rages, why it sweeps and gusts and levels.

Again, in another dream, an angry and questioning
wind asked if I had prayed, made an offering, and
why was I only remembering stories of harm? Did
I not remember the gentle birth of the wind, how
the great God in creation was lonesome for a like
spirit, made the wind to be the messenger for all
the world, to sing the beauty of rising energies.

Then I saw the gentle ground-wind pick up pollen
and spread it across the plants, watched as the warm
gentle breath from the south brought moisture for the
animals, while the lazy breeze from the east circled
back, one more time, with energy for the sky. Finally
a raging storm from the west forced waves of rain to
descend upon and cleanse earth of all evil and filth.

Sweet grass, cedar and sage had sent smoke to open
the minds of the two-legged, ignited a fire for electric
pulses, heated the rocks that speak the wisdom of
all directions. For us, the wind flies the entire world
by day and by night so that it will be everywhere at
once. For all this, the ones that ride the wind—the
swallow, geese, and hawk—sing grateful songs.

DRAGONFLY SUMMER

It was hot that day, horizon slowly evaporating,
whirlwind easing up dust tracks. Unexpectedly,
a large four-winged darted across my vision.

Cedar boughs, parted by a low summer breeze,
opened a path for the being from ancient times
to approach. To my arid senses the visit was a

wonder for this northern spirit. Bringing all its
power from distant skies, I saw in Dragonfly's
company the whirlwind and hail. It hovered

and fanned me with the scent of rain off distant
observing hills. A gentle humming stirred up
pure thoughts, a reference for the next hour.

I strained to hear its welcoming voice, those
whirring wings, a whisper in a dialect heard in
the womb. As it circled my place, a feeling of

humbleness and awe surrounded my breathing.
But in my heart I was rattled, yet I begged to be
included in this flight, this story. I wanted all

that distracts, that which binds my wandering
third spirit to disappear and let me go. I extended
a hand to the scent of southern cedars and beheld

as flight and speed became Dragonfly's ultimate
power. I wanted its essence to pass through me,
replenish my well of understanding. As Dragonfly

flew into the God of Wind, I watched its wings
and the wind become one, a stratum of crystal and
webbed veins. The distant storm was immediately

upon us, showering cedar with female rain reflecting
diffused lightening, turning collected moisture
into hail. I watched as the gods above motioned

Dragonfly to accept the gift of speed to dodge
harmful stones from Thunderbird's flexed talons.
In summer I was led to this consecrated event

when the Winged Nation retold the old stories on
the backdraft of summer storms. I inhaled and
exhaled the flight, and realized the favor of Dragonfly.

All that would try to confuse me, now will have
to find my wings. If harm looks for me, the quickness
of spirit will leave it behind and I will seek the realm

of cedar and offer songs to all Winged Nations.

FOUR

"Each of us is put here in this time and this place
to personally decide the future of humankind."

—*Chief Arvol Looking Horse*

AM I A WRITER OF THE WEST?

for my Grandfathers

I'm asked. Before I answer, I will get permission.
I have had this relationship with the West all my life.
It is the direction the Red Road has steered my
tracks since birth, where I learned the difference

between positive and negative, the place I sat in silence
astounded by thunder's education, and it is the last seat
before my final winters. All was approved by my elders
and was spoken in Dakota to my children and theirs.

Now the non-Indian wants to know if I am a writer of
the West. I tell you, I have permission and will share.
My writings are not mine: they are about being an
ancestral *Dakota/Lakota* human and living with the

Four Directions. I write about an ancient way, about the
two-legged who speak an old tongue, not English but
Dakota. I write about *woniya* (spirit), *wanagi* (ghosts)
and *takuskaska* (movement) rather than religion. When

I think about place, I think about *Dakota Macoce*, a
Dakota region, or *Makamibe*, the world of the common
man. I also see and feel where my four spirits converged,
became a two-legged to live within this sphere of complete

life. This portal, the place where I entered the surface of
Grandmother Earth's sacred breath, this convergence is
my place of entry into this realm. That area could be at a
latitude and longitude, or it could be a site of another name.

53

Where I was born is what I write about, it happens to
be an area that some call Montana or the West. I allow
myself to identify place the way I remember in my earliest
memory, or according to the cosmology of my cultural clock.

If that place is in accordance with the non-Indian's definition
of West, then we can talk. Now the thinking of my mind is
this place of writing could be inclusive with the non-Indian's
definition if they would understand my meaning of the West.

THAT THE FEAST MAY CONTINUE

for Dalton's family

The food blessed by the old gods from above and
below will feed relatives with tears yet streaming
in dark woods and behind sorrow blankets. Once
and again the higher gods see so much beauty in
the beginning souls of children, sometimes it is the
wish of webs and eternity to retrieve their breath
and guide them past struggles of binding times and
the weight of shut doors. They are taken for another
day, when Spring colors are blooming and open to
nurturing life. It is always the one who gives birth
who sees the sky abstaining above strained rivers
and torched grasses, the one who hears the whisper
of ghosts and accepts the untimely black shawl of
sad air and a heart wanting the awful beat to stop.
It has been a narrow granite road for twelve moons,
filled with shadows of slashed arms and cut hair.
Only until the renewing season will ceremony be
called back, when the chosen Sun Dancer with knots
of red cloth, carrying forth the sacred pipestone,
will healing prayers begin. Those beckoned to feed
grieving spirits step to the center of ritual, and those
of grace with healing cloth follow behind to wipe away
remaining tears. The weighted black shawl of sorrow
is replaced with a fresh shawl of restoration. The
sanctified food is shared with the shadowed spirit, and
in a last farewell, the living watch in wonder and joy
as the young spirit returns to the Milky Way. Those
who will continue to live with earth receive equal
plates of spirit food—their renewing energy. That
the feast may continue, relatives and friends take the
food back to their homes to be shared and celebrated
with more family in honor of the departed as he fulfills
his journey, in beauty, toward the Great Mystery.

ACKNOWLEDGE YOUR SOUL

for my father, James

He was always giving me a lesson. Sometimes he'd
begin and I would wonder where this one was leading,
but I never doubted, because what he was telling me

was out of love. Father was a very generous person
who strived to prepare me for life. He said I would find
out one day something about the people of this society.

They don't take care of their souls; they ignore their
spirit like they don't know how it works. He said they
forget how relevant it is. What he knew for sure was

that a lot of people will want to save my soul.
"Don't listen," he said, "They can't save your soul
because it belongs to God. It doesn't need saving.

It's their problem," he said, "They have a hard time facing
life and death because they have not taken care of their
soul." Wondering and timid, I knew I needed to listen

carefully to what he was saying. "One of our spirits is
our soul, the most important of our spirits." What he was
disclosing was pressing, all I could do was sit quietly.

"Other spirits join us when we come to live on this sacred
earth." Immediately, what came to my mind was one
particular ceremony Lala shared with us at the Round

House on the flats. One man had been seeing a ghost
around his barn, so the Medicine people prayed with
the man and his family. Lala had the people make a

circle around the man and his family, and asked that the ghost find peace and sleep. After that the man was not bothered, the ghost left him alone. "Our soul arrives with

us when we are born and leaves when we leave," Father said. "Acknowledge your soul and fill it up with all the good and wonderful things the Great Spirit gives us while

we are here on earth." He said it could be a beautiful sunrise, our children laughing and happy, all the birds returning and singing, and above all, thankful prayers.

GAME

Tracks are all that define these voices,
hungry lives pulsing sacred ground.
We are a journey of distressed shapes,
red essence on parchment, occupying a life.
We look for the fated four-legged that paced
this way, a tested and well-worn path
among storms, mud, into this shared hidden
brush. Coyote, slipping by through old
winter grass, warns in a pagan tongue,
licking after our scent. We pick up pace,
tighten our careless reins, snap back at the
yellow-eyed clown with throat hunger,
that gnawing bone that drives us on. Quieted,
we hear the heart beating. A desperate breath
crashes through dry branches, a silhouette
give away. In an instant we let go
of weapons and invite a quick death. We
watch our knives glistening. Obsidian
works for us. What image of blood on flesh,
odor of iron. A vermilion sun heavy with
spring looks upon reflections of death
in hard visions, our favorable hunt—
whitetail not quick enough for downwind
lessons. Our horses burdened, deer shadows
left on landscape, we push forward.
These tracks ours now. Game will heal all.
Our offspring dance, Grandmother prepares a
fire and sharpens another knife. During the
feast we thank any god absent from our table.

THE PASSING OF AN ELDER

They came from the sky where creation is nested, where endless stars partake in Great Spirit's precise plans and dreams for their journey. It is the time when a clear bright ray of satisfaction reflects from a place beside the Milky Way that the earthbound spirits come together to take their position for the journey: to walk the realm of earth in a sacred way. In human form, their life is full of instruction and ceremony, an image of beauty and respect. Their goal is to teach the children the sacred rituals of the Sacred White Buffalo, the mother of their past life. Each moon and each winter the Ancestors sing words for the paths they walk. Brothers and sisters of four-legs, the relatives of the winged, and those who live with water all welcome the new spirits and give in example their lives for food, shelter, warmth, and lessons of earth's good way. Each elder was told an old story for their use and safety, and in a never-ending circle, they share with their families. When so many sunrises and sunsets have shown waves of light to the old ones, they wait for one night to view the sky. On the spirit road they see their star brightening and remember the way back to the beginning. During the night we hear songs from ancestors heralding the moment of our elders' departure. We listen and acknowledge the songs of the cosmos as they welcome the scared ones back to the Milky Way. We are thankful that they lived, brought us life and shared the messages of the universe; in the final song we ask the stars to watch the temporary road, the one we walk now—our sacred earth.

FOR MYSELF

This day, I adorn braided
sweet grass earrings handed
down from Mother's *Santee*
rings of aromatic medicine.

From the ancestor lands of
Father's Lakota family, I fill
pockets with handfuls of
cedar, my protective shield.

Into this circle of morning
spirit food, a prayer surfaces
from the Southern recess of
primal night-dwelling dreams.

I thank the Western powers,
where a mirror reflects
images of the ones I trust—
transparent photos of the

Mitakuyepi, floating in
frames of red and yellow
buffalo grass, thundering in
a structure of immortality.

To my ancestors' Northern
power, my garden awaits
the first sound of thunder, I
meditate a promise of sage,

the offering to be burned,
waving away harmful spirits.
To the East where all our
ceremonies approach the

carved pipestone, I extol
all the waiting visible spirits,
"Thank you for this rising,
this keep that cradles me."

Santee: Eastern branch of the great Sioux Nation

THE DOLL WITHOUT A FACE

for granddaughter, Iehwatsirine

Not a stick figure
covered with moss, twine, clay,
but a shape well thought out,
created in the likeness of you and me.
Fine doeskin
to create the body, arms, legs, feet,
clothed with a fine fringed dress,
moccasins, leggings,
quillwork detailed and exceptional,
a belt, hair ties, necklace,
braids of horse hair, straight, thick.
The face and voice we remember
like Mother's gentle words about
how to treat people.
We see the strong hands of Auntie,
as she describes the speed of lizards
or the beauty of running horses.
We may want to see someone
singing songs of praise
about good hearts and good days.
It is always what we wish for.
This is what Auntie told us:
The doll has no face so we may
always see and hear who
we love, honor and remember.

I KEEP NEEDLES, BEADS . . .

for granddaughter, Iotshatenawi

I keep needles, beads, deerskin and sinew in tied-up
bundles under my bed, high on top of shelves, in near-

by dressers and rusty trunks where spirits of old women
and animals examine the colors and designs for the next

generation. I begin creating amulets from newly smoked,
fawn-skin, into shapes that resemble lizards that reach from

swampy water. They will be packed with delicate herbs
of sage, the kind that chase immoral spirits. Another shape

comes into being like the body of a doll, long dark hair,
red feet and hands, an apron with full pockets. I keep

this one wrapped in fragrant grasses that are pleasing
and sacred to all that is good in this world and beyond.

On the eve of all full moons the shapes take a step forward
in their creation—for my mood so full of energy and form.

I ordain the skins with energy exerted from living air and
prayer. Later, other designs will come to being, take

shape, will benefit from the tireless fingers that survived
all these long seasons. The designs that wait to live for

another day take their place in the shadows, with the ones
who came before, who stand guard. But the last works of

labor will progress slowly; we will never finish this piece.
As the old women remind us, "Keep busy, be thankful,

pray, lest we stare wide-eyed at the ending world for our
idleness, our waste, our inhumanity to all things created."

THE KNIFE WEARER

This morning we found ourselves skinning a deer,
cutting meat, hanging some to dry and packaging
some for the freezer. It was the dogs late last night

that set off a howling, the unexpected smell of fresh
blood floating down the block, then a familiar car
horn honking in the driveway. My nephew and his

friends were hunting and brought us a deer. Mother
always said, "Cut up the meat right away, don't let
it sit." I look at a front quarter, a hole filled with

coagulated blood. Grandma says not to eat the part
next to the wound, "Cut it out; offer it to the earth for
healing, a sacrifice to remember the hungering spirits."

Auntie says to save the muscle along the back strap,
"It makes good thread." I carefully learned the exact
place to cut the joints so the bones separate easily.

Mother said that is important—"It means you are a
thoughtful person." Auntie is at the door waiting for
a roast. "An elder takes the first piece," she reminded.

Mom tells me to save the hooves for her. She wants
to make a bone game for the new grandchild, wants
him to be patient and skillful. I boil the hoofs with

sage, find the little toe-bones for her. My hands begin
to ache from the work, I soak them in warm water
and start again. I admire the placement of tendons

on the deer shoulders, no joints, just the crisscrossing
of muscle. Grandma says, "That's why your dad called
them jumpers, they bounce off the strength of their

flexing muscles." Late at night Mom helps me stake out the hide. My back hurts; my feet feel like I've been walking on rocks all day. I want to complain,

but Mom catches the look in my eyes. She says to me, "When you get dressed for the dance this weekend, you will proudly wear your beautiful beaded dress,

your beaded leggings and moccasins, and last, but not least, you will put on your beaded belt, and attached you will wear your sharp knife and quilled knife sheath

because of what you have done this day."

SANENESS AND STONES

After leaving the concrete and dirty
air of a city gone mad for smoke and oil,
I came stumbling into this century on
weakened legs from years of alien
teachings, my head a giant fishbowl of
English words swimming backward, line
after line. Somewhere beyond the blurred
glass orb I was approached by even more
thieving users, excavating my cultural
mind, dried branches reaching for my
soul, their words a prairie fire kicked up
by an unforgiving inquisitive burn, forcing
me to the ground, licking my flesh with a
fixed flame. The intense heat left my core
a shade of blood I barely recognized, but
managed to spit out to keep from losing
the character guarded so carefully by
my eternal spirits. It was the ancient they
hated, the firmament of my beginnings
that puzzled them, the DNA they wanted
to analyze for their own wasted ashes. I
had to isolate what skin was left, hide the
children, cloak the elders, then plan for a
secure return when prayer and birth would
be safe. I dared not think of losing frontal
cortex, saneness a better option for the old
promise to stand. It was the stones that
sought me out, directed a path to earth's
womb for rebirth. I used fire for my own
benefit. Heated, the stones spoke about new
beginnings, safe places, and the lasting power
of hardening my shell, of waiting in silence.
Grateful for the old guard, I made a medicine
pouch full of tiny rocks for each step I walk,
each breath I take, each new saving heartbeat.

WICONI

for cousin/brother, Sonny

Air from the south presses into the last tissue of skin

left on our limbs. We live. After days of light reshaping,

deep nights restoring, we turn and take one last look,

dust off the lies that tried to absorb our good feelings,

tried to leave us with vengeful implants, tried to drown

culture. That journey attacked our will, stabbed at our

wiconi. We prayed, stood together, then raced away from

the infecting mud. The nerve, thinking they could send

their death to dance our children away, thinking they

could erase centuries of tradition. *Wiconi,* our good life

pulses our blood, defines our DNA, secures our spirits,

guides our shadows. We remember our trip from Milky

Way, the promise to the children, our reverence to White

Buffalo Woman, and the pledge of harmony with the earth.

We will not stop for evil. We will not honor the negative.

Our spirits will lead us safely to all that is sacred on earth.

Wiconi: The good way of life.

FIVE

"Here, in a fleeting quiet, I am awakened by the fluttering robe of the Great Spirit. To my innermost consciousness the phenomenal universe is a royal mantle, vibrating with His divine breath."

—Zitkala-Sa, *American Indian Stories*

I AM RELATED TO THE DAY

for my son, Neil

In this evolving evening hour, shades of red from
veins of sinking sun scatter among prairie grasses
   and along the curves of hills tinting all with rosy
   dust. I see silhouettes of *Mitakuyepi* move among

gray clouds of Grandfather's breath, the uplifting
of river fog to meet the voices of the coming storm.
   From everywhere they come, the flying ones with
   wings of rain from the West. They come hurriedly

like footsteps along the street. They come rattling
down the side of the house with water drops borrowed
   from the local river. I hear the new songs of young
   thunder, a fresh bird of Creator's making for now.

Minute after minute their breath shakes my thoughts
to join the family beings as their roars of joy echo
   in the flash of light, glaring from Thunderbird's eye.
   Again they come in a sacred way. They come close

with greetings from molecules I wear in my bones, a
light mist I recognize with my skin, a sweet trace of
   blessings signaling silence to leave and pores to open
   for surrender to this other world. They come, these

ancestors, these traditional relatives to wash our minds
and reasonings with a surplus of rotating constellations.
   These songs are translated from the backdraft of
   Grandmother, circling our thought-relayed language,

a reminder that we are still receiving wave after wave
of repast in dreams and godly meditations coming near.
Something sacred comes this way in hushed sounds
and calm, for the stones to awake and share their birth.

This day I consider mine, the gathering western spirits
have shown themselves, have called attention to what
we share, in time, and gladdened me with their walk
and harmony among my prayers, breathing and extent.

Mitakuyepi: Relatives in the D/Lakota language.

GRANDMOTHER THANKS WATER

Beckoning clouds
    to come her way,
Grandmother lifted
    her hands and
requested
    plentiful release
from bulging
    afternoon clouds.
Her garden space,
    created after the
first thunder, will
    benefit from the
millions of ion-laced
    rain drops
gently nourishing
    waiting seeds.
To the south, she
    knows *Mini Sose*
is filling, flowing,
    and gaining speed
as it bids good day
    to the storm.
She was served first,
    and she will harvest
for all the hungry,
    her promise to water.
She watches the sun
    settle into the river's
winding, glistening
    trail. In prayer,
Grandmother
    thanks water.

Mini Sose: Missouri River, also *turbulent water*

I PLAY A DRUM

for grandson, Liam

I play a drum for all my unborn children.
   Can you hear it?
A beat driven from the edge of a deerskin moon,
   vibrating into my breasts.
The delta at the curve of my spine sends red and
   more red corpuscles up
oxygen vines for the heart sac that keeps a life
   pure, sure and pumping a
sound through muscle, bone, and skin. The same
   drum concerted my dear
ones, taught them to recognize the tempo laid down
   in lines and spaces onto
a womb of parchment and sinew for their listening,
   instructing the forming
ear. Each trimester a ripe taste circled my tongue for
   each song, for each breath
as power grew and limbs reached a swim for a new
   dance. What will be required?
Hold close the additional spirit joined to the generous
   well of blood, feed
dreams, sense the ghost, rest during departing tides.
   Soon the pulse will
grow louder, a portal will roar open for a new day,
   a new drum will cross
the bridge for a life of playing its own kind of music.
   My heart beat? My drum?
Will sing on forever, with hope for all the children.

A FRAME OF REFERENCE

for my son, Dustin

"The content of the myths reveals that they probably originated
from the play of imagination on daily happenings rather than
from primitive man's direct contemplation of a tale."

—*Dr. Franz Boas, Anthropologist*

In this body, electric pulses are ceremoniously installed between
flashes of lightning, and the pure, vital energy reflecting from the
contributing, stormy sun.

We remember all the levels of life we blazed through to get here:
Creator's plan, an assembly of spirits, energies from the lesser gods,
and the breath of life.

It is a frame of reference in the blueprint of genes from ancestors
who knew the Creator in the past and along the seasonal orb of
the Milky Way.

I have examined the earth for traces of wounded blood, the kind
that come from taking a stance for all that has motion, our
contend to survive.

This soil will inherit my returning promises, to respect the
cleansing floods and the winds in all they have contributed
to earth this time around.

In dreams of the last remembered thoughts relayed from
neutrinos and atoms, I perceive all the shades of blazing
red and cobalt blue as they

take their place in my gathered sacred souls. Often the
elements under my skin absorb the trembling quicker
than I am able to decode.

Last night Grandmother thanked four bright stars in the
northern heavens for creating her womb. As she agreed,
she honors the sky people.

Her Nation will translate their beginnings in the cosmos;
earth their destination, a recollection with the Great Spirit,
lest some dispute.

SOMEWHERE BETWEEN

for nephew, Russ

Somewhere between faith and
   his cluster of
commitments, a common man
   inhales love for
his people as he begins his flesh
   sacrifice at the
sacred Sun Dance pole. He gulps
   moisture from
humid air and lifts his prayers to a
   southern wind asking
his dragonfly to use its speed and
   take him quickly
to the world where vision is caught
   in hope, where
sacrifice is recognized and his
   weakness turns into
a victory over all that is negative.
   The tethered ropes
hold firm jagged pieces
   of his body,
his crying heart, and solemn words
   for the two-legged,
the children of Mother Earth. "This
   dance is a thank
you for all that has been received,
   and it is
a prayer that the people will continue."

SUNSET SENSING SPIRIT

for my niece, Rosalie

I am watching evening sun
   push running shadows against
   the bold side of my strength,

the gradual process of the lesser
   god watching the elements of my
   ghost, soul, and breath unite. I

feel part of self moving toward
   spaces occupied by startled trees,
   where wooden fences want growth.

Sunset sensing spirit joins as a
   delightful ground wind enters and
   leaves the place where dress and

bone keep me camouflaged and
   standing. I sense a rising of thought
   as flowers nod. In anticipation,

eager buds, enjoying the speed of
   dragonflies, let scent loose. Plants
   pass photosynthesis to the glow of

my face, the shine of my hair, and
   cool the long radiating strands of
   heat off my image. As the pulsing

globe lowers, the four-winds soften
   the daggers of dying heat and join
   the pale murmurs of setting sun.

MOON OF CHANGE

Quietly, the sky shifts from blue
    to grey, air from warm to chilled.
        This morning as we head south to
our place of work, Canada geese
    race our clouds on their last run
for the midway climate of a lower
    state. We wonder. Their travel,
        a kind of prayer, a trusted gaze at
the angle of the decreasing light,
    a quiet belief in mountain draft,
depth of forest shadows, sheen
    off rivers and soft flow of fog.
        Inside our place of warmth, we
watch the chickadees that will
    stay, fluff feathers, look for deep
nests, watch the deer put on more
    fat, grow thicker coats, gophers
        carry off feathers, tufts of hair
and dying grasses for lining
    burrows. In unison, all prepare
for the shift in energy, temperature,
    and unite with the moon of change.

STORMS ABATED, THE PHOENIX SUN ACQUIRES

for grandson, Jett

Imagining a hope,
    a safety, so carefully prayed for and received—in exhaling relief—
for the chosen one, coming from the lower portion of the quadrant of
lakes, as he settles onto the desert of birth and rises to touch anxious
thoughts and half moons carefully planned and dreamed of.

Imagining from afar
    a lonely place below an imposed line separating my heart and spirit
from blood in another country, I count the hours between them all,
their spirits and my waiting lobes that will be quenched by a thirteen-year-
old song relayed as promised on air and in lines, assuring safety.

Imagining the hurried
    walk of several small footsteps, including an older, deeply set pair
running along concrete squares in a place of tall steel walls. These eyes
see far and in detail for the happiness of the four, birthed forty years after
my last child assumed the care for the next generation of descendants.

Imagining my thirst,
    each drop growing in size as a bird lets go a kind of miniature roar
of water for a waiting spirit and an open heart. Only the all-knowing,
blazing feathers of Phoenix can fan a cloud of good news for this old,
tired brow who's praising the magic of flight and safe landing.

MARRIAGE

Among the tall thick leaves of muskrat
food, dragonflies busy selves supping
stout vanilla flowers resting high off the
watery paths and still green shallows of
Tule Creek. Into this far location hidden
in reeds and cattail, mallards have made
their flight to settle, forever bond, and
attentively care for each and their young.
Reflections of pond and sky inhabit the
jade neck feathers of the handsome, noble
Drake, always guarding, keeping a circle
of safety. The elegant female always mindful,
always cared for, knows her brown foliage
means camouflage. They will secretly raise
the ducklings to maturity, to assure that
they know the gift of returning, of existence.
In ceremony, the plumage of the Drake was
tied to my husband's feather braid for his
dedication to family—in following example.

WE WAIT NEAR WATER

They come after midnight
        where food grows on water
        aligned with sun,

A flight repeated by
        dark birds, sun-colored eyes,
        planned for centuries.

The male red wings
        return first, find nesting areas,
        next moon, females.

Men, calloused hands,
        strong-muscled arms, hack and
        burn interior wood.

Every season
        the river sings for new canoes,
        a smooth gliding.

We hold place close,
        grass grabs ions filled with fire,
        then autumn.

Songs among throats,
        we all watch how buds arrive,
        grow with day and air.

After the blazing heat
        staple of grain sprouts easily
        for earth's rotation,

Birch bark baskets ready,
        enter swamps, beat stalks gently
        for wild rice.

COME WITH ME

for cousin/brother, Jack

In my early waking hours, I see you, Cousin, putting on
special traveling moccasins, the kind with four blue wings

extending from the flutter of your feet. You ask me to race
with you, south with the restoring light, while the sun is low,

past old blood of silent stones waiting to proclaim our flight
into the arms of our family homelands where Mother's heart

reflects off summer stars. I have been dreaming, sometimes
in deep sleep, sometimes in distant longings, and when

the sweet smell of mint tea floats among kitchen curtains.
The dream is always remade to entice my yesteryear play,

you hold my hand through our running and discovery, to share
our findings of turtles, or cocoons with our elders, then

to receive their nods of approval. I see shapes of far hills,
like the profiles of men in our clan, cloaked in a mist of deep

thought and prayer after departing showers of a storm. I see
sunlight through edges of opal clouds offering spears of sacred

light on the faces of busy women as they up-earth the soil for
tasty new roots among hills covered in velvet flowers and healing

medicinal herbs. The sound coming is always the same: a
uniting of deep male voices and high pitched trills from female

throats ignited by electric branches that vibrate from low male
thunder into my brain stem and up into the cortex of my early,

waking dream. It is always, Cousin, apparitions of our four-legged relatives carrying our people to a gathering of our sacred selves.

Always, the dream calls me. It calls all clan members whose blood recalls gusting air and quick flight that can take us there.

You ask me to inhale my dream, make it my path, partake in fulfilling the future and wake to the call of blue dragonflies.

LOIS RED ELK is an enrolled member of the Ft. Peck Sioux in Montana, with roots from the Isanti on her mother's side, and the Hunkpapa and Ihanktonwa from her father, who is descended from the Sitting Bull family. Raised in her traditional culture, she is a quill and bead worker, a traditional dancer, and an advocate for cultural preservation and practice.

During her earlier years, living in Los Angeles, she was a TV talk show host at KCOP-TV, an FM radio host at Pasadena City College, and a technical advisor for many Hollywood film productions. She has been a member of Screen Actors Guild and the American Federation of Television and Radio Artists for forty years while working for all the major networks and Hollywood studios in film and television.

She enjoys writing poetry, prose and children's stories and has been published in many Native American anthologies and poetry magazines. As a freelance writer she worked for her tribe's Native newspaper and authored a weekly column titled "Raised Dakota."

Presently she is on the adjunct faculty at Ft. Peck Community College, Montana, teaching cultural arts courses she developed, including Traditional Plants, Domestic Arts, Animals Significant to Dakota Culture, and Porcupine Quill Work.

She and her husband, who is enrolled in Shawnee, Oklahoma, have been married for forty-five years. They have two children, eight grandchildren and one great grandchild.

Her first book, *Our Blood Remembers,* was published in 2011 (Many Voices Press) and won the Best Poetry Award from Wordcraft Circle of Native Writers and Storytellers.